WordPress FOR STUDENT Writing Projects

GRADES 6 – 12

Complete Lessons Aligned with
Common Core Standards for ELA

Erik Bean, EdD
Emily Waszak

COMPASS

WordPress for Student Writing Projects

Copyright © 2014 by Erik Bean and Emily Waszak

Published by Brigantine Media
211 North Avenue, St. Johnsbury, Vermont 05819

Cover and book design by Jacob L. Grant

Brigantine Media/Compass Publishing
211 North Avenue
St. Johnsbury, Vermont 05819
Phone: 802-751-8802
Fax: 802-751-8804
E-mail: **neil@brigantinemedia.com**
Website: **www.brigantinemedia.com**

ORDERING INFORMATION

Quantity sales
Special discounts for schools are available for quantity purchases of physical books and digital downloads. For information, contact Brigantine Media at the address shown above or visit **www.brigantinemedia.com/compass**.

Individual sales
Brigantine Media/Compass Publishing publications are available through most bookstores. They can also be ordered directly from Brigantine Media.
Phone: (802) 751-8802; Fax: (802) 751-8804; **www.brigantinemedia.com/compass**.

ISBN 978-1-9384063-4-8

CONTENTS — □ ✕

Student blogs are a great vehicle for helping students in middle school and high school learn collaborative writing skills, and WordPress software is a great tool for creating student blogs. As a way to share written work, student blogs can facilitate such writing processes as: brainstorming, writing, rewriting, developing theses, preparing arguments, editing, fact checking, and more. WordPress blogs can be used in many ways to sharpen your students' writing and reinforce Common Core writing standards. Each lesson in this book includes one or more assessment rubrics that show the specific Common Core writing standards met. Appendix C details the writing standards for grades 9 - 12 and outlines the way teachers can put those standards into operation in the classroom.

WordPress blogs can be used to engage students in a variety of different kinds of writing: informational text essays with tracked online research, creative writing pieces such as short stories and poetry, or journalism pieces, including entire school newspapers. In this book, you'll find lessons to help you teach writing skills using WordPress, along with examples from several teachers who have used WordPress blogs successfully with their students.

Some of the benefits of incorporating WordPress blogs into your writing instruction include:

▷ Posting student writing on the class WordPress blog makes the written pieces available for the whole class to read, critique, and help revise.

▷ WordPress blogs contain built-in discussion threads where teachers can have control of what information is posted and who can comment. Student discussions can be tracked and graded. Students can be online at the same time and work together on a project, or they can contribute to the critiquing process outside of school time. Teachers can collect student opinion about an article or the quality of a source.

▷ WordPress is free software, another plus for classroom use. The code used by WordPress is universally available and can be modified as necessary. There are numerous optional WordPress plug-ins that add features to spark creative writing and critical thinking.

Familiarize yourself with WordPress, using the "Getting Started" steps in Appendix A (**page 32**). Once the blog is created and you are comfortable navigating around WordPress, you're ready to start working with your students on a blog project.

You'll need a computer and monitor. An LCD projector or similar device is also needed to display the blog to the whole class.

You may need to update your browser to be sure that your blog will be easy to use. Most browsers work well with WordPress as long as they are up-to-date. Many experienced WordPress users recommend Mozilla Firefox as the browser of choice (**http://en.forums.wordpress.com/topic/which-browser-is-the-best**).

After your students' pieces are written, you will post them to the class WordPress blog where they will be available for the entire class to read. If you want to share your students' work with parents, administrators, or other teachers, a WordPress blog makes it easy to do.

PRIVACY/PRECAUTIONS

While no social network is one hundred percent safe, using WordPress with your exclusive domain address can meet most privacy concerns. You supply the web address only to students, staff, and parents. However, any site on the Internet has the potential to be seen by outsiders. Students should not include their last name in any postings, but adding a last name initial can help differentiate between students whose first and last names might be the same. As an added precaution, WordPress pages can be password-protected. If you want to obtain parental permission, Appendix B (**page 35**) is a form that you can tailor for your district or school.

This WordPress blog project is an essay assignment about each student's hero. The subject matter works well to engage students and encourage student feedback, collaboration, and analysis. This Hero Essay project is appropriate for grades six through twelve. Learning outcomes include recognizing heroic figures in the media, analyzing literature for the heroic archetype, and thesis development and support. See accompanying rubrics (**page 13**) for assessment and Common Core Standards alignment.

TEACHER PREPARATION: approx. 1 hour —□X

Set up your class WordPress blog, if this is the first time you are using it. Appendix A (**page 32**) details the steps.

Before the students' essays are due, build one new WordPress page for each student. The new pages will automatically include a text box field and a comment area (similar to those found on Facebook and other sites).

CLASS DISCUSSION: 25 minutes —□X

1   Start with a class discussion about heroes. Ask students if they have a hero. Ask them to define a hero. You will get different definitions because heroes mean different things to different people.

2   Ask students to choose someone they consider to be a hero. For this assignment, their hero should be a well-known person. For example, a hero may come from the world of sports, politics, science, business, entertainment, religion, or another public sphere.

3   Each student is to write about the hero's most meaningful societal contribution based on electronic published evidence. Students should develop a claim or thesis that includes two heroic personality traits tied to their hero's most meaningful societal contribution. Students should write in the third person voice.

4   Distribute Hero Essay Parameters (**page 9**) to each student. If you use a digital means

to distribute assignments, post the Hero Essay Parameters on that vehicle as well as the class WordPress site. If you prefer, the Hero Essay Parameters can be printed and distributed to each student.

NOTE:
The evidence produced by students to back up their choice of hero will be hyperlinked to each student's WordPress reference page. This electronic linkage will create an evidence trail that classmates can examine.

HERO ESSAY PARAMETERS

Word Count: 600 to 800 for grades 6 - 8
800 to 1,000 for grades 9 - 12

Choose a hero to write about. Select a famous person for whom information is available online. Write your essay as a Word document.

INTRODUCTORY PARAGRAPH

1   Begin with a stimulating lead sentence about heroes in general.

2   Explain why heroes are important (two or three sentences based on your own critical thinking). You may wish to use an analogy or short anecdote.

3   Develop a thesis that includes two personality traits tied to the most meaningful societal contribution your hero has made. Be sure that within your piece you include hyperlinks to the evidence you have discovered to back up your claim that this person can be considered a hero.

BODY

1   Give the hero's background: date of birth, education, family, career milestones, and hurdles. Keep in mind that accomplishments alone do not make a hero.
(one to two paragraphs based on reliable sources)

2   Describe the hero's most meaningful contribution: explain the most prominent impact the hero has made on society. Why is the hero a role model? For example, did the hero help create a new industry and provide jobs? Does the hero give hope to a particular group of people? Emphasize the hero's most significant contribution(s).
(one paragraph)

3   Describe the hero: define the hero's personality.
(two paragraphs)

4   Tie the hero's personality traits to the hero's most meaningful societal contribution.
(one paragraph)

CONCLUSION

Sum up the hero's personality, accomplishments, and why the chosen hero is a role model.
(one paragraph)

1. After you have given your students the Hero Essay assignment parameters, introduce the WordPress blog. Explain that the word "blog" is short for "Web log" and is an online diary. Display, on a big screen if possible, the initial WordPress page you have created. Explain that after they complete writing their essays, the essays will be published on the new class WordPress blog, which will allow each student to collaborate or discuss the essays.

2. Explain the collaborative process. When students' essays are completed, they will be posted on unique WordPress pages, one for each student. Each student will then visit the class WordPress site to read each essay. Students will provide feedback in comment fields below each essay. All student feedback must be constructive, not destructive. This feedback period will occur over several days. Through the collaborative process of posting student comments in WordPress, the entire class will participate in the writing, editing, and rewriting process. Each student will be graded on both his or her essay as well as the quality of his or her feedback. The WordPress blog will leave a permanent trail of comments and essay revisions. Positive feedback from other students will provide motivation and boost student confidence. Students will see their writing flourish over time.

3. Choose the amount of time you will allow for writing the first draft of the hero essay and give your students the time frame. Make sure students understand that the WordPress collaborative process will help them revise their first drafts into more complete essays.

4. Have students write their first draft essays electronically and send them to you via e-mail.

When students e-mail their first drafts to you, post them: copy and paste each essay to its individual student page. You may have to adjust spacing between paragraphs after you paste in the essay. Press the "publish" button and the essay will be online. Repeat this process for each student essay.

COLLABORATION DAY

After all the essays have been posted to the blog, it's time for students to collaborate on their work. Collaboration Day is exciting! It represents the completion of your students' initial drafts and showcases the new WordPress blog.

TEACHER PREPARATION: 10 minutes — □ ✕

Put the WordPress blog on the big screen in your classroom before the students come in, if possible.

CLASS DISCUSSION OF THE COLLABORATION: 30 minutes — □ ✕

1   Explain the collaboration process that each draft will undergo: writers collaborate with peers to examine the word choice, plot, sentence construction, clarity, and meaning.

2   To help ensure that each student understands how to critique and collaborate within the WordPress comment fields, select one of the essays you found particularly note-worthy. Ask a student to volunteer as a peer editor. As peer editors, students have two responsibilities:

    – Point out to the author those things that he/she does well.
    – Point out to the author what he/she could do to improve the piece.

Explain that the only acceptable criticism is constructive, not destructive, and that being too simple should always be avoided. For example, students should never just write "good essay" or "nice thesis." The goal is to hone in on what the author did right or should consider re-writing.

3   Have a student read the first paragraph of the chosen essay aloud.

4   Have the volunteer peer reviewer post his or her critique to demonstrate the process. The post may not be immediately visible. A message may indicate the post is awaiting approval from you, the site moderator. If this occurs, once you have logged into the site, select "Comments" along the left column. Approve the comment. You can decide later if you want to allow all comments to be published without approval.

5   Repeat this initial collaborative comment process using another student volunteer to critique another portion of the essay, such as the body or the conclusion. The indi-vidual whose essay is being critiqued should not defend why he/she wrote a particular sentence, paragraph, thesis, or any other portion of the essay under review. Focus here on how to comment appropriately.

6   Assign each student five essays from other students to read and post comments. You choose if these will be done in class or as homework.

MONITOR STUDENT CRITIQUES: Variable time frame

1. After the collaboration process starts, you need to monitor and respond to the comments. During the first couple of days of collaboration, discuss the collaborative process with the class and point out the type of comments that are helpful.

   Examples of appropriate comments: "Thanks for your analysis." "Very good lead!" "Excellent thesis variables." "Needs more hero background information." Have students focus on a particular section of the essay, such as the introduction, and provide feedback about that part of the work. Help students understand that *specific* feedback allows their peers to benefit most from the collaborative critique process. For many, peer criticism may be a new concept.

2. The critique period can continue in class or at home for the time you allot. Once all critiques are completed, each student should carefully examine the WordPress collaborative feedback to create his/her final draft. Students should address only those peer-posted comments that they think will help them better meet the assignment rubric. They should also address any comments made by the instructor.

POST FINAL ESSAYS: 30 minutes

After students have revised their essays to final form, add them to an additional student page in the WordPress blog.

ASSESSMENT

Two rubrics are included for grading purposes:

- Assessing first drafts and final essays (**page 13**)
- Assessing quality of student collaborative critiques (**page 16**)

SUGGESTIONS FOR GRADING STUDENT COLLABORATION:

Since the back end of your WordPress site includes statistics, check these to see which users contributed comments and count the frequency based on their User IDs. In addition, examine the comment history of each essay to see who commented and check the rigor of those comments.

RUBRIC 1 - ESSAY WRITING (DRAFT AND FINAL)

Student Name: _______________________   Date: _______________________

Writing Variable	1-4 Needs Work	5-6 Fair Job	7-8 Good Job	9-10 Terrific	Score	Common Core Strand	
Thesis	Thesis is not clear. Reads like an editorial.	Thesis mentioned with one variable, but not well developed.	Thesis is clear and contains at least two variables.	Thesis has well-defined variables and expressed authoritatively.		W.9-12.1 W.9-12.2 W.6-8.1	W.6-8.1a W.6-8.2 W.6-8.2a
Evidence	Points are confusing and not connected to main topic.	Average development of points presented.	Evidence is presented well; needs fine-tuning.	Points are valid, plentiful, clear, and concise.		W.9-12.1 W.9-12.2 W.9-12.7 W.9-12.8 W.9-12.9 W.6-8.1 W.6-8.1b W.6-8.1c W.6-8.1d	W.6-8.2 W.6-8.2b W.6-8.2c W.6-8.2d W.6-8.2e W.6-8.7 W.6-8.8 W.6-8.9 W.6-8.9b
Argument	Not at all convincing.	Somewhat convincing; needs more support, facts, and evidence.	Convincing, but needs fine-tuning.	Excellent presentation, very convincing, strong development of argument to support thesis.		W.9-12.1 W.9-12.2 W.6-8.1 W.6-8.1b W.6-8.1c W.6-8.1d	W.6-8.2 W.6-8.2b W.6-8.2c W.6-8.2d W.6-8.2e W.6-8.9b

RUBRIC 1 - ESSAY WRITING (DRAFT AND FINAL) P.2

Student Name: _______________________ Date: _______________________

Writing Variable	1-4 Needs Work	5-6 Fair Job	7-8 Good Job	9-10 Terrific	Score	Common Core Strand	
Details	Minimal details offered.	Details in developmental stage.	Details are good; the reader has a feel for the stance the writer has taken.	Details are vivid, strong, and embrace the reader; the argument is convincing based on the details supporting it.		W.9-12.1 W.9-12.2 W.6-8.1 W.6-8.1b W.6-8.1c W.6-8.1d	W.6-8.2 W.6-8.2b W.6-8.2c W.6-8.2d W.6-8.2e
Conclusion	Summary not clear and concise; introduces new information; does not reiterate thesis.	Summary in development stage; needs work.	Decent summary, but could be stronger.	Summarizes, does not introduce new information, reiterates thesis.		W.9-12.1 W.9-12.2 W.6-8.1 W.6-8.1c W.6-8.1d	W.6-8.1e W.6-8.2 W.6-8.2d W.6-8.2e W.6-8.2f
Vocabulary	Very limited range of word use; utilizes slang and/or attacks.	Some development of word variance evident; slang and/or attacks evident.	Vocabulary is at grade level; good use of variety of words and expressions.	Highly effective in using a variety of words; avoids attacks, slang, etc.		W.9-12.1 W.9-12.2 W.6-8.1 W.6-8.1a W.6-8.1c W.6-8.1d	W.6-8.1e W.6-8.2 W.6-8.2b W.6-8.2c W.6-8.2d W.6-8.2e

RUBRIC 1 - ESSAY WRITING (DRAFT AND FINAL) P.3

Student Name: ___________________   Date: ___________________

Writing Variable	1-4 Needs Work	5-6 Fair Job	7-8 Good Job	9-10 Terrific	Score	Common Core Strand	
Grammar	There are more than 15 serious grammar errors.	There are 10 – 15 serious grammar errors.	There are fewer than 10 serious grammar errors.	There are no serious grammar errors.		W.9-12.1 W.9-12.2 W.6-8.1 W.6-8.1a W.6-8.1c W.6-8.1d	W.6-8.1e W.6-8.2 W.6-8.2b W.6-8.2c W.6-8.2d W.6-8.2e
Mechanics/ Spelling	There are more than 15 errors in spelling, capitalization, punctuation, and end marks.	There are 10 – 15 errors in spelling, capitalization, punctuation, and end marks.	There are fewer than 10 errors in spelling, capitalization, punctuation, and end marks.	All sentences use correct spelling, capitalization, punctuation, and end marks.		W.9-12.1 W.9-12.2 W.6-8.1 W.6-8.1c W.6-8.1d	W.6-8.2 W.6-8.2c W.6-8.2d W.6-8.2e

RUBRIC 2 - COLLABORATION

Student Name: _______________________ Date: _______________________

Writing Variable	1-4 Needs Work	5-6 Fair Job	7-8 Good Job	9-10 Terrific	Score	Common Core Strand	
Blog Entry	Met 50% or less of blog entry requirement; low quality of feedback.	Met 75% of the blog entry requirement; moderate quality of feedback.	Met the blog entry requirement; quality of feedback is decent.	Exceeded the blog entry requirement; quality of feedback is strong.		W.9-12.1 W.9-12.2 W.9-12.4-6 W.6-8.4	W.6-8.5 W.6-8.6 W.6-8.10
Cohort Support	Did not make an appropriate effort with peers in class or electronically.	Made a minimal effort with peer support in class or electronically.	Worked well with others; demonstrated support of peers in class or electronically.	Offered extra support to those peers in need in class or electronically.		W.9-12.1 W.9-12.2 W.9-12.4-6	W.9-12.10 W.6-8.4 W.6-8.5

Use your class WordPress blog to teach students how to write a thesis. This lesson concentrates on the value of constructing quality claims and arguments while refuting fallacies. This Thesis Writing project is appropriate for grades six through twelve. Part One involves learning to write thesis statements. Part Two extends the lesson by adding Internet research on the thesis topic and learning how to recognize quality research sources.

PART ONE - CREATING THESIS STATEMENTS

TEACHER PREPARATION: 10 minutes   — □ ✕

Create a new WordPress page (the thesis landing page) for the purpose of thesis writing practice before you start the lesson.

CLASS DISCUSSION: 25 minutes   — □ ✕

1. Discuss the concept of a thesis with your students. One definition that works for this project: **a thesis is a summary of a proposition that will be upheld in an essay.** The thesis is usually the last sentence in the introductory paragraph. Explain that it is important to take a side on the issue, but remind students to write the thesis in third person so the writing speaks with authority.

   The following example shows a thesis with and without at least two thesis variables tied to something meaningful. Since the objective is to write about issues that are well published, a thesis with no variables does not often examine the most prominent issues for debate.

   Editorialized thesis with no variables: "Michigan should repeal its mandatory motorcycle helmet law."

   – This thesis is void of variables and is not tied to anything meaningful. Although this thesis has a third person voice, it does not contain sufficient information to build a robust essay offering specific and/or relative subject information currently debated in published texts.

Non-editorialized thesis with well-defined variables: "If Michigan repeals its mandatory motorcycle helmet law, the state may earn several million dollars in travel, restaurant, and healthcare revenue."

– This thesis contains three variables: travel, restaurant, and healthcare. It is tied to something meaningful – revenue.

You can tailor the level and sophistication of theses to meet your class and department needs.

2   Students can develop thesis ideas by visiting the "Freshly Pressed" WordPress blog, a round up of "editor's picks to community favorites" located at **http://en.wordpress.com/fresh**. This page features new blog releases and often includes a wide array of human interest or newsworthy stories and commentaries. Have the students examine the variety of blogs. Each student should choose a topic that is controversial or newsworthy.

3   After your students have read the blog of their choice and found more information on the Internet regarding the subject, have them navigate to your WordPress thesis landing page and post a general title for that topic in the available comment form. If you enable "no moderation" for comments, they will post immediately.

4   Under the student's topic, each student posts a preliminary one-sentence argumentative thesis. Students can use the WordPress comment field for writing and rewriting until they feel their thesis is ready to be published on the site.

COLLABORATION FOR THESIS DEVELOPMENT: 25 minutes 

1   Have students help each other develop their theses via the collaborative process discussed in the Hero Essay project (**page 11**). Encourage students to critique at least two or three peer theses.

2   Have students post links related to their thesis on a "Resources" WordPress page so every student can acquire background information on each topic. Students can easily copy and paste a Web address into the WordPress comment field. They also can include a few words about why they were attracted to the story.

ASSESSMENT 

Once the collaboration has been closed, use the rubric (**page 19**) to grade the initial preliminary thesis as well as the peer feedback.

RUBRIC 1 - THESIS DEVELOPMENT

Student Name: _________________________   Date: _________________________

Writing Variable	1-4 Needs Work	5-6 Fair Job	7-8 Good Job	9-10 Terrific	Score	Common Core Strand	
Thesis	Thesis is not clear. Reads like an editorial.	Thesis mentioned with one variable, but not well developed.	Thesis is clear and contains at least two variables.	Thesis has well-defined variables and expressed authoritatively.		W.9-12.1 W.9-12.2 W.6-8.1	W.6-8.1a W.6-8.2 W.6-8.2a
Argument	Not at all convincing.	Somewhat convincing; needs more support, facts, and evidence.	Convincing, but needs fine-tuning.	Excellent presentation, very convincing, strong development of argument to support thesis.		W.9-12.1 W.9-12.2 W.6-8.1 W.6-8.1b W.6-8.1c W.6-8.1d	W.6-8.2 W.6-8.2b W.6-8.2c W.6-8.2d W.6-8.2e W.6-8.9b
Evidence	Points are confusing and not connected to main topic.	Average development of points presented.	Evidence is presented well; needs fine-tuning.	Points are valid, plentiful, clear, and concise.		W.9-12.1 W.9-12.2 W.9-12.7 W.9-12.8 W.9-12.9 W.6-8.1 W.6-8.1b W.6-8.1c W.6-8.1d	W.6-8.2 W.6-8.2b W.6-8.2c W.6-8.2d W.6-8.2e W.6-8.7 W.6-8.8 W.6-8.9 W.6-8.9b

RUBRIC 1 - THESIS DEVELOPMENT P.2

Student Name: _______________________   Date: _______________________

Writing Variable	1-4 Needs Work	5-6 Fair Job	7-8 Good Job	9-10 Terrific	Score	Common Core Strand	
Details	Minimal details offered.	Details in developmental stage.	Details are good; the reader has a feel for the stance the writer has taken.	Details are vivid, strong, and embrace the reader; the argument is convincing based on the details supporting it.		W.9-12.1 W.9-12.2 W.6-8.1 W.6-8.1b W.6-8.1c W.6-8.1d	W.6-8.2 W.6-8.2b W.6-8.2c W.6-8.2d W.6-8.2e
Vocabulary	Very limited range of word use; utilizes slang and/or attacks.	Some development of word variance evident; slang and/or attacks evident.	Vocabulary is at grade level; good use of variety of words and expressions.	Highly effective in using a variety of words; avoids attacks, slang, etc.		W.9-12.1 W.9-12.2 W.6-8.1 W.6-8.1a W.6-8.1c W.6-8.1d	W.6-8.1e W.6-8.2 W.6-8.2b W.6-8.2c W.6-8.2d W.6-8.2e

RUBRIC 1 - THESIS DEVELOPMENT P.3

Student Name: ___________________   Date: ___________________

Writing Variable	1-4 Needs Work	5-6 Fair Job	7-8 Good Job	9-10 Terrific	Score	Common Core Strand	
Grammar	There are more than 15 serious grammar errors.	There are 10 – 15 serious grammar errors.	There are fewer than 10 serious grammar errors.	There are no serious grammar errors.		W.9-12.1 W.9-12.2 W.6-8.1 W.6-8.1a W.6-8.1c W.6-8.1d	W.6-8.1e W.6-8.2 W.6-8.2b W.6-8.2c W.6-8.2d W.6-8.2e
Cohort Support	Did not make an appropriate effort with peers in class or electronically.	Made a minimal effort with peer support in class or electronically.	Worked well with others; demonstrated support of peers in class or electronically.	Offered extra support to those peers in need in class or electronically.		W.9-12.1 W.9-12.2 W.9-12.4-6	W.9-12.10 W.6-8.4 W.6-8.5

PART TWO - RESEARCH TO SUPPORT THESIS

This lesson helps students learn to use research to defend a thesis or create more arguments and claims. Students will examine what constitutes a quality source of information, and then use their quality sources to make arguments defending their theses.

TEACHER PREPARATION: 15 minutes 

Set up a WordPress landing page dedicated to research sources and claims.

CLASS DISCUSSION: 25 minutes

1   Begin a discussion about sources, their quality, and inherent biases.

2   Ask students if they know the various biases that even a reputable source could contain. Discuss how a source's affiliation fundamentally leads to bias.

3   Explain that, for the purposes of this assignment, no more than twenty percent of the sources used to support a thesis should be more than five years old. Quality sources can include reputable news sites such as CNN.com, ABCNews.com, or NPR.org. You can feature these sites on your WordPress home page. Lead the students to library databases such as EBSCO, ProQuest, or ERIC that feature a mix of peer-reviewed and mainstream quality articles culled from journals, magazines, and newspapers.

RESEARCH SOURCES AND CLASS POLL: 25 minutes 

1   Conduct a poll of your students' opinions on sources, asking students to vote on the quality of each source, using a scale of 1 to 5 (5 as the highest quality source). For more information on creating a poll for your class WordPress site, visit **http://wordpress.org/plugins/wp-polls**.

2   Inform the students that when you close the poll, you will remove the lowest polled sources and have students replace them with better quality sources. Decide as a class how many of the lowest polled sources you will remove. Continue the quality source discussion on the polling page.

STUDENT POSTS AND COMMENTS ABOUT SOURCE QUALITY:
25 minutes - several class sessions

1   Have each student post claims and arguments regarding why his/her chosen source exhibits quality. These should be simple one-sentence claims that assert a prominent supposition.

2 After each student has posted one claim defending why the source is considered a quality source, allow other students to critique the quality of these assertions. Make sure students have honed in on the value of the claim.

After the collaboration period has ended, grade the work using the rubric (**page 24**).

RUBRIC 2 - THESIS RESEARCH

Student Name: _______________________ Date: _______________________

Writing Variable	1-4 Needs Work	5-6 Fair Job	7-8 Good Job	9-10 Terrific	Score	Common Core Strand
Argument	Not at all convincing	Somewhat convincing	Convincing	Excellent		W.9-12.1 W.9-12.2 W.6-8.1 W.6-8.1b W.6-8.1c W.6-8.1d W.6-8.2 W.6-8.2b W.6-8.2c W.6-8.2d W.6-8.2e W.6-8.9b W.9-12.1
Cohort Support	Did not make an appropriate effort with peers in class or electronically.	Made a minimal effort with peer support in class or electronically.	Worked well with others; demonstrated support of peers in class or electronically.	Offered extra support to those peers in need in class or electronically.		W.9-12.2 W.9-12.4-6 W.9-12.10 W.6-8.4 W.6-8.5

The purpose of this assignment is two-fold: (1) to strengthen the student's perception of the connection between reading and writing, and (2) to strengthen the student's ability to express personal thought/opinion about the topic in a text. The student needs to be able to read a text, understand its content well enough to summarize it in writing, and then share his/her own ideas about the topic. The response should answer questions such as: "Do I agree/disagree with the author's point?" "Do I have a similar experience to share?" "How would I respond if I was involved with the problem?" This project helps to improve reading comprehension, sentence construction, and paragraph writing. It combines both third person and first person writing. It is an engaging exercise for grades six through eight.

This lesson satisfies numerous Common Core standards as noted in the accompanying assessment rubric (**page 27**).

TEACHER PREPARATION: 10 minutes

Set up a new landing page (a new main page) for this lesson. You can create one new WordPress page for each student or use each student's existing page and add this one. If you retain the existing WordPress individual student pages, they become the students' archives of class assignments.

CLASS DISCUSSION: 25 minutes

I   Have the students locate an Internet news story that was published the year (or the day) they were born. Stories should be controversial, to allow for discussion and thought about the topic.

How to find appropriate news articles:

While a Google search may yield some articles, a trip to your school's library or media center is recommended. If your school subscribes, a good place to start searching for news articles is via Gale/Cengage Publishing's *InfoTrac Newsstand* database. Junior and high school editions are available. This database specifically features stories, articles, and access to a number of periodicals from 1980 through today. Students begin the search by specifying the month, day, and year. For example, if you choose January 23, 1999, the results will yield more than 7,000 stories from major newspapers the world over. In the left column, you can choose the most prominent periodicals such as the *New York Times* and the *Washington Post*. The complete articles can immediately be read online or emailed to the student directly as text or in PDF format. If your school does not have access to this database, check with your school media specialist for other database subscriptions that may yield similar results.

2 Each student should email his/her chosen news story to the teacher. Make sure each student retains a copy of the chosen story in digital format, text or PDF.

POSTING STORIES: 30 minutes 

Post the news stories to each student's WordPress page by copying and pasting the text version of the article. Since most databases where students will find their stories are not accessible to the public, posting the link alone is not sufficient. Another option is to print the stories and distribute them to every student. Add the name of the student who chose the story to each copy.

STUDENT WRITING: 50 minutes 

1 Using a word processing program, students write and then post to their WordPress page both an article summary and a response paragraph. Remind the students:

   – The summary paragraph should mention the author of the story and its title.

   – It should summarize the most prominent story theme and sub-themes, if applicable.

   – The summary paragraph should be written in third person voice and should highlight any major statistics, facts, or decisions made.

   – The response paragraph can be written in first person and should discuss what the student would do if confronted with the problem.

2 You can allow collaboration on this project. Ask each student to visit other peer pages and comment on whether they agreed with the original news writer's story in general, if their classmate's summary was accurate, and whether their classmate's response met the objectives.

ASSESSMENT 

Use the rubric (**page 27**) to grade students on the quality of their summary and response paragraphs, as well as their comments to other students' writing.

RUBRIC - BIRTHDAY NEWS

Student Name: _______________________   Date: _______________________

Writing Variable	1-4	5-6	7-8	9-10	Score	Common Core Strand
Cohort Support	Did not make an appropriate effort with peers in class or electronically.	Made a minimal effort of peer support in class or electronically.	Worked well with others; demonstrated support of peers in class or electronically.	Offered extra support to those peers in need in class or electronically.		W.9-12.1 W.9-12.2 W.9-12.4-6 W.9-12.10
Conclusion	Summary not clear and concise; introduces new information; does not reiterate thesis.	Summary in development stage; needs work.	Decent summary, but could be stronger.	Summarizes, does not introduce new information, reiterates thesis.		W.9-12.1 W.9-12.2 W.6-8.1 W.6-8.1c W.6-8.1d W.6-8.1e W.6-8.2 W.6-8.2d W.6-8.2e W.6-8.2f
Vocabulary	Very limited range of word use; utilizes slang and/or attacks.	Some development of word variance evident; slang and/or attacks evident.	Vocabulary is at grade level; good use of variety of words and expressions.	Highly effective in using a variety of words; avoids attacks, slang, etc.		W.9-12.1 W.9-12.2 W.6-8.1 W.6-8.1a W.6-8.1c W.6-8.1d W.6-8.1e W.6-8.2 W.6-8.2b W.6-8.2c W.6-8.2d W.6-8.2e

RUBRIC - BIRTHDAY NEWS P.2

Student Name: _______________________   Date: _______________________

Writing Variable	1-4	5-6	7-8	9-10	Score	Common Core Strand
Grammar	There are more than 15 serious grammar errors.	There are 10 – 15 serious grammar errors.	There are fewer than 10 serious grammar errors.	There are no serious grammar errors.		W.9-12.1 W.9-12.2 W.6-8.1 W.6-8.1a W.6-8.1c W.6-8.1d W.6-8.1e W.6-8.2 W.6-8.2b W.6-8.2c W.6-8.2d W.6-8.2e
Mechanics/ Spelling	There are more than 15 errors in spelling, capitalization, punctuation, and end marks.	There are 10 – 15 errors in spelling, capitalization, punctuation, and end marks.	There are fewer than 10 errors in spelling, capitalization, punctuation, and end marks.	All sentences use correct spelling, capitalization, punctuation, and end marks.		W.9-12.1 W.9-12.2 W.6-8.1 W.6-8.1c W.6-8.1d W.6-8.2 W.6-8.2c W.6-8.2d W.6-8.2e

Teachers have found innovative ways to use and adapt these WordPress lessons. Here are three examples of real teachers and how they are using WordPress in their classrooms to teach writing in a variety of ways.

Karen Salsbury, a seventh grade English language arts teacher in the North Kansas City School District, changed the Hero Essay assignment to an argumentative one that she called, "My First Essay," and introduced the initial collaborative nature of WordPress blogs in draft form only. Students selected essay topics based on their personal interests. One student wrote about the history of horror films and another wrote about Google Fiber, **http://eastgatemsela.wordpress.com/?s=fiber**, a fiber-optic Internet service.

Salsbury was chosen by her district to test the use of iPad minis to bring technology into the classroom, and this initial WordPress site lesson put the devices to good use. While her spring 2013 site did not elicit the type of collaborative feedback the essay lesson can yield, the use of WordPress created a forum to inspire critical thinking. Salsbury is preparing to focus on the Hero Essay in Spring 2014 and plans to infuse the rigor of collaboration.

Salsbury has learned that her students enjoy using technology and finds that using WordPress is a great way to keep them attentive and on task. She also welcomes the fact that parents are easily able to view the site and see what their students are working on and monitor their writing progress.

Salsbury estimates that it took approximately one hour to set up the WordPress site and fifteen minutes to create user names that were routed to student email addresses for approval. Posting essays and student comments took approximately one hour.

Scott Earl, Temperance-Bedford High School AP English Literature Instructor and Bedford Literary Guild Advisor in Monroe, Michigan, created a WordPress site called Kicking Mule Writers, named after Bedford High School's mascot – Maximus, the Kicking Mule. It is located at **http://kickingmulewriters.wordpress.com**. Writing and posting fictional stories and poetry as blog items satisfies Common Core Standards W.9-12.3, which cover narrative forms of writing, either real or imagined, as well as W.9-12.4-6, which address production and distribution of writing.

Earl set up 27 pages on WordPress (one for each of his students), using each student's first name and last initial as the sub-URL. For example, a student whose name is Adam J. has a Web page with this address: **http://kickingmulewriters.wordpress.com/adamj**. If additional student privacy is required, a numbering system can be used for the individual blog posts.

After his students had been working on their short stories and poems for about a week, Earl posted their work. Earl then made each member of the class a "user" of WordPress. A user has some commenting privileges but cannot alter the site as an administrator can.

Students were allowed to post throughout the entire WordPress site using their user name. Students could also share the site with their friends and family.

Each student was required to provide comments to five peers. As peer editors, students had two responsibilities:

1   Point out to the author those things that he/she does well.

2   Point out to the author what could improve his/her piece.

Earl gave the students guidelines for poetry and for short stories as follows:

For poetry:

–Specific, vivid word choice – tell them what word is weak, offer a replacement suggestion

–Form – are they following the form? Does the rhyme scheme seem forced, making the poem's meaning less clear?

–Clarity – is it clear what the poem is about?

For short stories:

–Believability/plausibility – does the plot make sense? Even if it is science fiction, does the plot make sense? Does one thing lead to another?

–Sensory images – does the author take you there?

–Dialogue – is it realistic? Does it move the story along, or does it get in the way?

Earl estimates that he spent approximately one and one-half hours of preparation time for this project, including setting up the WordPress blog and posting the short stories and poems to the blog.

TO TEACH JOURNALISM

Several high schools, colleges, and universities use WordPress to create online editions of their school newspapers. ***The Eagle Eye, Online Edition***, a product of Lock Haven University, Lock Haven, Pennsylvania, is a great example of an electronic college newspaper using WordPress as the delivery platform. Dr. Sharon B. Stringer, *The Eagle Eye* news advisor, is in charge of the electronic edition.

Student reporters write the stories and then funnel them to one student who edits and posts the stories. Anyone with a WordPress ID can post comments, which are currently unmoderated.

Like a typical newspaper, the most newsworthy or prominent stories are published on the home page and most contain a hyperlink to lead the reader further into the publication. Producing an online edition of the newspaper allows alumni and other members of the Lock Haven University community to have access to the newspaper at a manageable cost.

The Eagle Eye, Online Edition can be shared on Facebook, Twitter, and Flickr. With more than 1,000 Facebook likes, it is clear the flexibility to incorporate social networking for the print and online WordPress edition is a way to increase readership. WordPress also allows stories to be shared on other social networking sites, such as LinkedIn and Pinterest.

There are numerous middle and high school online newspaper sites created with WordPress. Examples of successful sites include: *The Branford High School Buzz*, from Branford, Connecticut (**www.branfordbuzz.com**), *The Prowl Newspaper*, from Palmetto High School in Palmetto, Florida (**prowlnewspaper.wordpress.com**), and *The Blotter*, from New Albany High School in New Albany, Indiana (**nahsblotter.wordpress.com**).

An electronic WordPress newspaper is time consuming, but, in many cases, the production of the newspaper is part of a journalism class. At least ninety minutes is needed to set up the initial WordPress site. Artwork such as the masthead or flag need to be designed separately and added to the site. It is also necessary to set aside several hours of instruction on journalistic concepts to encourage objective story writing and reporting. Student editors will spend several hours each week to write, edit, re-write, post, and encourage other students to submit articles.

There are three categories of users of WordPress blogs:

A   bloggers who sign up to build a Website blog

B   users who sign up to post comments to blogs

C   followers who can view and get updates on any number of WordPress blogs.

PROCEDURES 

WordPress offers two types of websites: one, where bloggers who have more sophisticated html knowledge can build a website by downloading special WordPress website software, and two, at WordPress.com, where a less experienced blogger can point and click to establish a blog Web address and create a site.

REGISTERING TO CREATE A BLOG 

The following steps will help you navigate the simpler, non-html process to get your blog established.

1   Point your browser to **www.WordPress.com**.

2   On the home page, click "Get Started."

3   Supply your email address, and below it, the WordPress system will automatically include a username based on your email. You can change it to something easier for you to remember. No one but you will see your username.

4   Choose a password based on strength.

5   Create a blog address. This name should be easy to remember and relate to your blog subject. For example, if your high school name is Central High, you could choose

"CentralHighWriters.WordPress.com." The blog address is not case-sensitive.

6   The WordPress site will analyze if your blog name is available, and if it is available with a popular domain name ending such as .com, .me, or .net. If it is available under a popular domain name ending and you choose that ending, you will be charged an annual domain fee as noted on the WordPress site. If you use the default WordPress domain name ending of "WordPress.com" (for example CentralHighWriters.Wordpress.com), there is no fee to register. This is the domain name ending we recommend.

7   Click "Create Blog" when you have decided on your blog name. You will see a confirmation that an e-mail has been sent to the address you provided. It may take up to 30 minutes to receive the confirmation link in your e-mail.

8   Log on to the e-mail address you provided and find the e-mail from WordPress. Click the link, "Activate Blog."

9   Your new WordPress blog site is now live with its initial first page publicly available. Have one browser page open to the new blog site in addition to the browser page you are using to log on to the site. By toggling back and forth, you can see the progression of pages added and any changes made on the back end.

10 Go back to the WordPress.com home page and login into your new blog with the User ID and Password you created earlier. (If you are the sole owner of the computer you use to create your new WordPress site, we recommend you first bookmark the WordPress.com login page and title the bookmark with your User Name and ID to help you remember it.)

11 In the upper left portion of the horizontal menu bar, select "My Blog," or click on "1 Page" near the center of your screen. This will take you directly into the backend of the blog.

12 Click "Appearance" along the left column menu to select your theme. There are many choices, and you can view them A – Z, the most popular themes, new themes, and themes that are "trending." Some themes are only available to be purchased, which is noted below the theme's name, with the cost. "Premium" themes are only available for purchase.

13 Each template can be previewed. Think carefully which style best reflects your school and writing blog purpose. Click "activate" below your chosen template to permanently install it.

14 Some templates have more sub-template choices. If your template choice does not immediately activate, it could be due to the security settings of your browser. Refresh your browser to see the new theme in place.

15 Customize the menu links you want available. Include an announcement that the blog is now under construction for your class by navigating to "Pages" inside your WordPress backend dashboard.

16 Your class is now ready to begin publishing!

REGISTERING TO BE A WORDPRESS USER   —□✖

Each student should sign up as a "user" of WordPress. By signing up as a user under a pseudonym, students can contribute to the site and remain anonymous to the general public. In order to register, the student must have a valid e-mail address. Many school systems provide one. If the student does not have an e-mail account, consider having them sign up for a free Gmail or Yahoo account. Register for WordPress by supplying a valid e-mail address for confirmation at **https://signup.wordpress.com/signup/?user=1**.

REGISTERING TO BE A WORDPRESS FOLLOWER —□✖

Parents, faculty, and administrators who might benefit from examining your WordPress class site can become followers. To be a follower, visit a WordPress blog you wish to track. In the lower left corner you will see a gray rectangular "Follow" box. Click it to enter a valid e-mail address. Once you click the confirmation link, you will receive alerts each time someone makes a new post. Every time you become a WordPress follower and confirm via e-mail, you will be taken to your WordPress follower page, where you can select or deselect any of the blogs you have tracked.

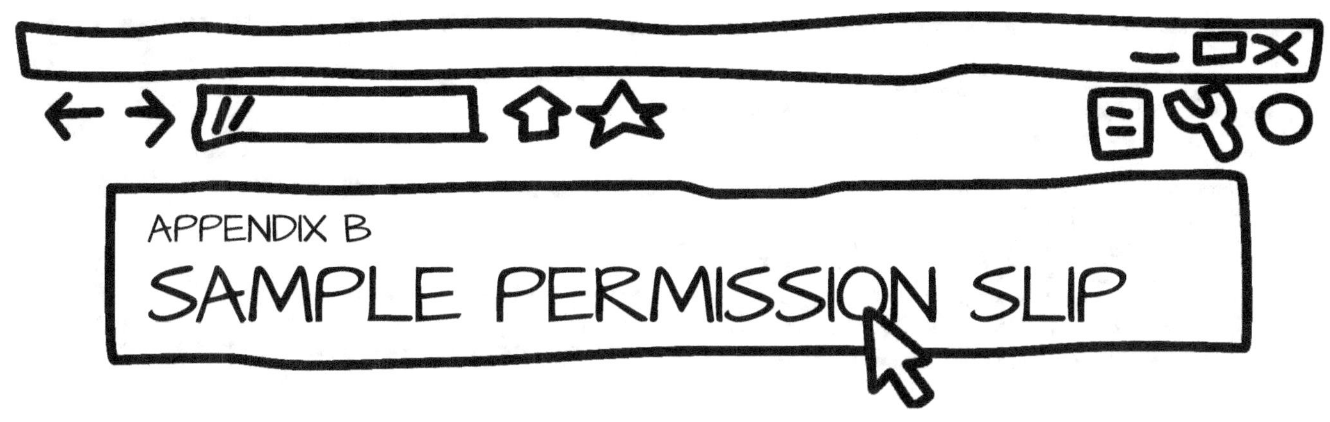

Date: _______________________

To Whom It May Concern:____

The _____________________________ School District prides itself on innovative educational opportunities for students to learn in a variety of different ways. Recently several institutions have begun to incorporate lesson plans using social media since so many students and faculty alike enjoy the venue. We would like your permission to create a WordPress account on behalf of your child for use in writing exercises tied to the Common Core.

Only the instructor, your child, and other students in the class will participate in the writing exercises through WordPress. Only your child's first name or a pseudonym will appear in the discussions. While no social media network is one hundred percent safe, we have taken every precaution to ensure only the faculty member and students will share in the learning exercises that will take place during class and occasionally in the evening for homework, if required.

Your signature will allow your child to participate immediately:

_________________________________   _______________________   ____________________

Please print name   Please sign   Date

Once your approval is received, your child will be furnished with a WordPress unique site name. Parents are encouraged to log on and monitor the lessons by clicking the "follow" button and confirming via e-mail. Please have your child return the signed slip as soon as possible to his or her English Language Arts instructor. Thank you for your cooperation and we look forward to a great new learning experience!

Sincerely,

THE ENGLISH LANGUAGE ARTS TEAM

The CCR anchor standards and high school grade-specific standards work in tandem to define college and career readiness expectations—the former providing broad standards, the latter providing additional specificity. Below each Common Core Standard are specific ways that secondary school teachers can put the standards into operation using the lessons in this book. Common Core Standards for grades 6 - 8 are very similar to those for grades 9 - 12, and the ideas shown here will work for those grades, as well.

TEXT TYPES AND PURPOSES 

W.9-12.1 Write arguments to support claims in an analysis of substantive topics or texts, using valid reasoning and relevant and sufficient evidence.

> **W.9-12.1a** Introduce precise, knowledgeable claim(s), establish the significance of the claim(s), distinguish the claim(s) from alternate or opposing claims, and create an organization that logically sequences claim(s), counterclaims, reasons, and evidence.
>
>> –Establish an argument on a subject matter.
>>
>> –Develop and revise a thesis statement.
>>
>> –Use pre-writing strategies to logically sequence ideas.
>
> **W.9-12.1b** Develop claim(s) and counterclaims fairly and thoroughly, supplying the most relevant evidence for each while pointing out the strengths and limitations of both in a manner that anticipates the audience's knowledge level, concerns, values, and possible biases.
>
>> –Defend a claim utilizing facts and statistics.
>>
>> –Identify social networking audience for which these claims are targeted.
>>
>> –Identify the audience.
>>
>> –Remain sensitive to the diversity of readers.
>
> **W.9-12.1c** Use words, phrases, and clauses as well as varied syntax to link the major sections of the text, create cohesion, and clarify the relationships between claim(s) and reasons, between reasons and evidence, and between claim(s) and counterclaims.

−Write a well-organized essay using standard grammatical syntax to link support-
ing ideas to thesis statement. For example, students will address sentence variety
appropriately placed words, phrases, and clauses to defend their position.

W.9-12.1d Establish and maintain a formal style and objective tone while attending to the
norms and conventions of the discipline in which they are writing.

−Create tone representing a non-bias, authoritative, third person voice. Avoid col-
loquial language, attacks, and slang, germane to the conventions of the argument.

W.9-12.1e Provide a concluding statement or section that follows from and supports the
argument presented.

−Write a conclusion that summarizes the major claims discussed in the body, without introducing new information. Reiterate thesis first.

W.9-12.2 Write informative/explanatory texts to examine and convey complex ideas, concepts,
and information clearly and accurately through the effective selection, organization, and analysis
of content.

W.9-12.2a Introduce a topic; organize complex ideas, concepts, and information so that
each new element builds on that which precedes it to create a unified whole; include
formatting (e.g., headings), graphics (e.g., figures, tables), and multimedia when useful
to aiding comprehension.

−Present a subject of their choice based on chronological, top/down, bottom up,
or historical significance via segments that collectively communicate a thorough
understanding.

−Present important ideas and/or facts about the subject in other forms of communi-
cations other than writing.

W.9-12.2b Develop the topic thoroughly by selecting the most significant and relevant
facts, extended definitions, concrete details, quotations, or other information and
examples appropriate to the audience's knowledge of the topic.

−Practice working on signal phrases (Diana Hacker, *Developmental Exercises for
Rules for Writers*, 2011) that introduce paraphrases or quotes to qualify the information for the reader, explaining its significance assuming the audience has little
or some basic knowledge of the subject.

W.9-12.2c Use appropriate and varied transitions and syntax to link the major sections
of the text, create cohesion, and clarify the relationships among complex ideas and
concepts.

−Develop sentence variety by using a combination of long and short sentences
to establish better readability as well as use conjunctions and coordinates and
occasional semi-colons or chronology with much more concentration on sentence
construction started in the first informative learning outcome

W.9-12.2d Use precise language, domain-specific vocabulary, and techniques such as
metaphor, simile, and analogy to manage the complexity of the topic.

–Use terminology or nomenclature appropriate to foster an authoritative writing tone.

W.9-12.2e Establish and maintain a formal style and objective tone while attending to the norms and conventions of the discipline in which they are writing.

–Copy edit the various paragraphs, sentences, and selected nomenclature until the entire informative topic is appropriately conveyed.

W.9-12.2f Provide a concluding statement or section that follows from and supports the information or explanation presented (e.g., articulating implications or the significance of the topic).

–Write a conclusion that aptly reiterates the major facts and importance of the topic.

W.9-12.3 Write narratives to develop real or imagined experiences or events using effective technique, well-chosen details, and well-structured event sequences.

W.9-12.3a Engage and orient the reader by setting out a problem, situation, or observation and its significance, establishing one or multiple point(s) of view, and introducing a narrator and/or characters; create a smooth progression of experiences or events.

–Examine multiple points of view – from first or third person limited to third person omniscient. Here students will embody idiosyncratic nonfictional, anecdotal, or fictional story telling through the use of rich and vivid character development and descriptive adjectives expressed in current, future, or past time sequences based on a conflict, plot, and setting.

W.9-12.3b Use narrative techniques, such as dialogue, pacing, description, reflection, and multiple plot lines, to develop experiences, events, and/or characters.

–Introduce dialogue or narrative that represents required story segments such as historical background, time sequence, and the major story theme tied to the protagonist, antagonist, flat (no effect on story outcome), and round characters (can effect story outcome).

W.9-12.3c Use a variety of techniques to sequence events so that they build on one another to create a coherent whole and build toward a particular tone and outcome (e.g., a sense of mystery, suspense, growth, or resolution).

–Focus on organization that adds to the creation of tone and purpose. Sequencing events will enhance a specific tone. For example, if creating a mystery, the writer will intentionally plant clues for the reader to follow.

–Focus on vocabulary and sentence variety by using a combination of long and short sentences to establish better readability. Separate them by using conjunctions and coordinates and occasional semicolons or chronology. Think about delivering a top-down or bottom-up explanation where appropriate.

W.9-12.3d Use precise words and phrases, telling details, and sensory language to convey a vivid picture of the experiences, events, setting, and/or characters.

–Use sensory imagery to portray plot, setting, and character.

W.9-12.3e Provide a conclusion that follows from and reflects on what is experienced, observed, or resolved over the course of the narrative.

–Create a logical and appropriate resolution.

PRODUCTION AND DISTRIBUTION OF WRITING   — ☐ ✖

The lesson plans provided in this book satisfy the Common Core strands listed below.

W.9-12.4 Produce clear and coherent writing in which the development, organization, and style are appropriate to task, purpose, and audience.

W.9-12.5 Develop and strengthen writing as needed by planning, revising, editing, rewriting, or trying a new approach, focusing on addressing what is most significant for a specific purpose and audience.

W.9-12.6 Use technology, including the Internet, to produce, publish, and update individual or shared writing products in response to ongoing feedback, including new arguments or information.

RESEARCH TO BUILD AND PRESENT KNOWLEDGE — ☐ ✖

W.9-12.7 Conduct short as well as more sustained research projects to answer a question (including a self-generated question) or solve a problem; narrow or broaden the inquiry when appropriate; synthesize multiple sources on the subject, demonstrating understanding of the subject under investigation.

> –Investigate a subject of the student's choice or teacher-generated by researching sources. This could range from simplistic problem-solving to synthesis of multiple sources.

W.9-12.8 Gather relevant information from multiple authoritative print and digital sources, using advanced searches effectively; assess the strengths and limitations of each source in terms of the task, purpose, and audience; integrate information into the text selectively to maintain the flow of ideas, avoiding plagiarism and overreliance on any one source and following a standard format for citation.

> –Judge the quality of a source. As students continue to conduct secondary research it is particularly important to examine the age, reputation, and in some cases, the peer review nature of juried published articles.

W.9-12.9 Draw evidence from literary or informational texts to support analysis, reflection, and research.

> –Extract specific evidence and draw conclusions based on the evidence.

W.9-12.9a Apply grade level Reading Standards to literature.

> –Use knowledge of periods of American literature to identify similar themes between the different periods.

W.9-12.9b Apply grade level Reading Standards to literary nonfiction.

> –Evaluate nonfiction primary source documents. For example, if students analyze the Declaration of Independence, they can examine form and structure in addition to understanding how logos, ethos, and pathos contribute to meaning.

RANGE OF WRITING 

W.9-12.10 Write routinely over extended time frames (time for research, reflection, and revision) and shorter time frames (a single sitting or a day or two) for a range of tasks, purposes, and audiences.

> –Perform a variety of writing tasks, such as writing an impromptu essay, creating a research paper, or writing a personal narrative or reflective analysis. Students should understand the processes to complete each type of assignment.

ACKNOWLEDGMENTS 

Special thanks to Bobbi Gutman, 40-year veteran Detroit area public high school English teacher, Claire Coffman, ELA seventh and eighth grade teacher, St. Peter's Catholic School, Clarkston, South Carolina, and Andrea Gumble, ninth and eleventh grade English teacher and department chair, Chenango Forks Central School District, Ithaca, New York, who assisted in operationalizing the Common Core Writing Standards. Also, many thanks to Karen Salsbury, Scott Earl, and Earl C. De Mott, whom we continue to work with utilizing other social networks for current and future projects.

www.ingramcontent.com/pod-product-compliance
Lightning Source LLC
Chambersburg PA
CBHW080506030726
47592CB00011B/3268